THE EARLY STONES

Legendary Photographs of a Band in the Making 1963–1973

Photographs by Michael Cooper
Foreword and Commentary by Keith Richards
Text by Terry Southern

Originated and Compiled by Perry Richardson

 HYPERION

New York

Photographic Archives Storage and Reproduction by Adam Cooper
Edited and Designed by Sandra Choron
Project Coordination: Mary Ann Naples

Library of Congress Cataloging-in-Publication Data

Copper, Michael, d. 1973.
    The early Stones : legendary photographs of a band in the making, 1963–1973 /
photographs by Michael Cooper ; foreword by Keith Richards ; interviews by Terry
Southern ; compiled by Perry Richardson.
        p.   cm.
    ISBN 1-56282-876-2
    1. Rolling Stones.   2. Rolling Stones—Pictorial works.   3. Rock
musicians—England—Portraits.   I. Southern, Terry.
II. Richardson, Perry.   III. Title.
ML421.R64C63   1992
782.42166'092'2—dc20   92-10232
                                               CIP
                                               MN

Produced by Rapid Transcript, a division of March Tenth, Inc.
Associate book production: Patricia Marcinczuk, Folio Graphics Co., Inc.

FIRST PAPERBACK EDITION

10 9 8 7 6 5 4 3 2 1

THE EARLY STONES

A C K N O W L E D G M E N T S

there are many people who've helped to make this book possible, but in particular the authors would like to thank Bert and Marlon Richards, Roy Martin, Tony Russell, Janet-Elen Richardson, Gail Gerber, Silvia Cooper, John Dunbar, David Courts, Tony Lacey, Chris Kewbank and Catherine Turner of the Special Photographers Company, Chris and Sue Hutton, Chuck and Susan Zuretti, Earl McGrath, Brian Clarke, Sandy Lieberson, Christopher Gibbs, John Brown, Sarah Janson, and George and Linda Segal.

Also, Allen Klein and Abcko Films Inc., *Vogue* magazine and Condé Nast Publications Ltd., and the Robert Fraser Foundation.

Finally, we'd like to thank Tony White and Joy Pester of White & Black Ltd., London, for producing such consistently superb prints of the photographs.

F O R E W O R D

by Keith Richards

So we were on a winner after all?"

I knew how good Michael was from the work of his that I'd already seen, but half the time never really imagined that there'd be film in the camera, let alone that it might be in focus. I mean, some of the states we got into, I don't think I could have picked up a guitar and played—and he was looning as much as any of us—but he was also working.

I find it hard to recall a lot of things about Michael. He had this extraordinary quality: He could be there and he wasn't there. Even my recollection of actually first meeting Michael is very strange.

It had to be at his studio. I went around there with Anita and Brian and Robert Fraser, in Kings Road. "Oh, let's stop off and see Michael," they said.

Michael was the first one who got me interested in photography. We would say, "What are you doing, Michael? Come on, we've got to go, man."

"No, I've got to do this, first I've got to do this," he'd say. We would try to rush him, but he was a photographer and he made it obvious that that's what he did.

I got interested in what Michael did just for the pure mechanics of it, the process. And hanging with him as a friend. We'd want to go eat but couldn't because something to do with photography preempted the plan. It was always, "We can't go now because bla-bla-bla takes this much time to process, bla-bla-bla." So I got interested while I waited for him. I'd ask, "What are you going to do next?" "Well, you've got to do this, and then develop and then shade it here, and then you sit out there and listen to the sounds," he'd say. Or, "Come into the darkroom and I'll show you." So I'd go into the darkroom, and he'd show me bits of what he did and I'd just watch. Soon I got more interested in Michael than in his photography, and it was only much later on that I began to see the results of his work and what he was on about, what he was trying to do, and I still see those things.

So he was always around. Sometimes I would say song." "Oh, can I come and watch?" he'd ask. to understand that anybody else would be Michael never presumed, never got in your way. taking pictures—was a natural part of the someone putting a camera in your face or making That's what he did. And it was very natural for there I could ever stand. He was always a hell of a

to him, "Stay a minute; I'm going to finish this "Well, if you want to." You always find it very hard interested in watching somebody else work. But He knew when to lay back, so what he did— relationship. He never bugged you; it wasn't like you self-conscious. Michael just took pictures. Michael to be around and to be the only person guy. It wasn't that you liked him so much that you

allowed him to do things that you wouldn't allow others to do; you were never even aware that he was doing it. That's what Michael did, and he did it so well and so naturally that no one was aware half the time that they were being recorded.

Then there was the great sounds connection. Great sounds—maybe that's another reason why we hit it off right away. It was like never leaving your own house—he had the same records I had! And he had this "jiggle dance" he'd do to "Dictionary of Soul"

and Otis—Otis Redding was his great favorite. But Michael was also a catalyst; he put an incredible number of people in touch with each other. I mean, he'd go to L.A. and I'd get a call from someone straight afterwards or even while he was there—Bruce Connors and all that lot Michael put me on to. He'd take someone round to Robert's, and after he'd gone Robert would come out with something like "Well, I'd just like to know what that chap's background is—was he in the Guards?" and Michael would say, "Are you kidding?! You didn't know that was so and so, son of Lord Bla-bla?"—and Robert would say, "What?! What?! Why didn't you tell me? Could at least have laid on a bit of a spread!" So, I mean, Bob had that sense of hierarchy, whereas Michael was just amused by it. I mean, he was aware of it, but it was sort of "Surely nobody can take that seriously!"

So Michael would take the lowliest of us, you know—talking about my people, my band, the lower strata—and put me in touch with some very hip aristocrats! Michael was really like the go-between— excellent name for him—between everybody. "That guy should meet so and so," he'd say. "He doesn't really know too much and he should really meet that guy, or so and so." He did that to everybody. In that sense he was far more revolutionary than British political agitators or flash-in-the-pan types; he put people in touch. Then he photographed it all! It must have been something like "I'd love to put this one in touch with this one and then photograph it!" Although, I don't really think it was quite as designed as that. It was just the way he was; it was part of him. I think he may have been aware of it to a certain extent, but he certainly didn't seem to be planning or plotting in a deliberate sense—it was just a very natural thing that he did.

Then there were the record covers, *Sgt. Pepper's* for the Beatles, *Satanic Majesties* for us. I can just imagine Michael sitting looking at his record collection one day, getting pissed off and thinking, "Hmmm—I could do better than those covers—maybe do one for the Beatles and one for the Stones." I mean, I know that's not quite how it came down, especially with *Sgt. Pepper's*, but he did do one right after the other, and no one said, "Are you kidding? The Beatles

and the Stones? Can't have that, they'll just be too similar." But no one even thought about that, and he did end up with the two covers to put at either end of his record collection!

The other thing about Michael was that he'd also spiral into deep depressions as well—almost like extra depths of depression about his personal life, for one reason or another, which would normally and usually turn out to be temporary, and like a few days later you'd see him and it'd be "Ahh—fine again."

There was a strange similarity between Brian and Michael. Not that they both died so young or so close together, but there was this sort of potentially bottomless depression to which they both seemed vulnerable. It was like some sort of supersensitivity that could rise up and claim them at any time. Brian's death will always remain suspicious. As for Michael, there was a time there around 1973 when everything seemed to have disappeared down the plughole, and I know that on top of that he was incredibly depressed about his personal life. But the real tragedy of Michael is that if he'd just managed to hold on a little bit longer, he could have sorted out his personal problems and he'd have seen things starting to come around again.

It was impossible to be with Michael for any length of time and not get turned on to his life as he got turned on to yours. After a while you'd start seeing things through his eyes. I'd say, "Look at that—get a picture of that"—an old lady getting into a cab or a boy sitting on a windowsill—and he'd say, "Oh yeah, right." So you'd start looking at things. I mean, he turned me on to always looking at the odd little scenario in the street, and he devoted that same level of ability, intensity, and skill to capturing the making of the Stones. Who couldn't be grateful?

The photographs in this collection go from '63 to '73 with just about every stop in between. Stu, Brian, Anita, Andrew Oldham, Mick, and me writing our first songs; recording at Olympic; people who influenced us; shooting what today would be called videos; getting busted; going to places like Morocco, Tangiers, Marrakesh for the first time; moving to the south of France; coming up with some of the songs; early tours; first tours to the States; playing to tens of thousands of people.

Just this last tour we were playing to something like one hundred and fifteen thousand in Prague, Czechoslovakia—and they hadn't quite sorted out the passport situation at Border Control with Poland. People were backed up for miles waiting to get out. But if you had a ticket to the Stones concert, you just waved it at the barriers and walked straight through—better than a visa! And you see, Michael caught the spirit of how this came to be—how it developed for the Stones. It's here in these photographs, which are really, in that sense, almost a piece of history—well, of our history anyway! It's Michael's record of the record of the making of a rock 'n' roll band. Hope you enjoy it!

—Keith Richards
1992

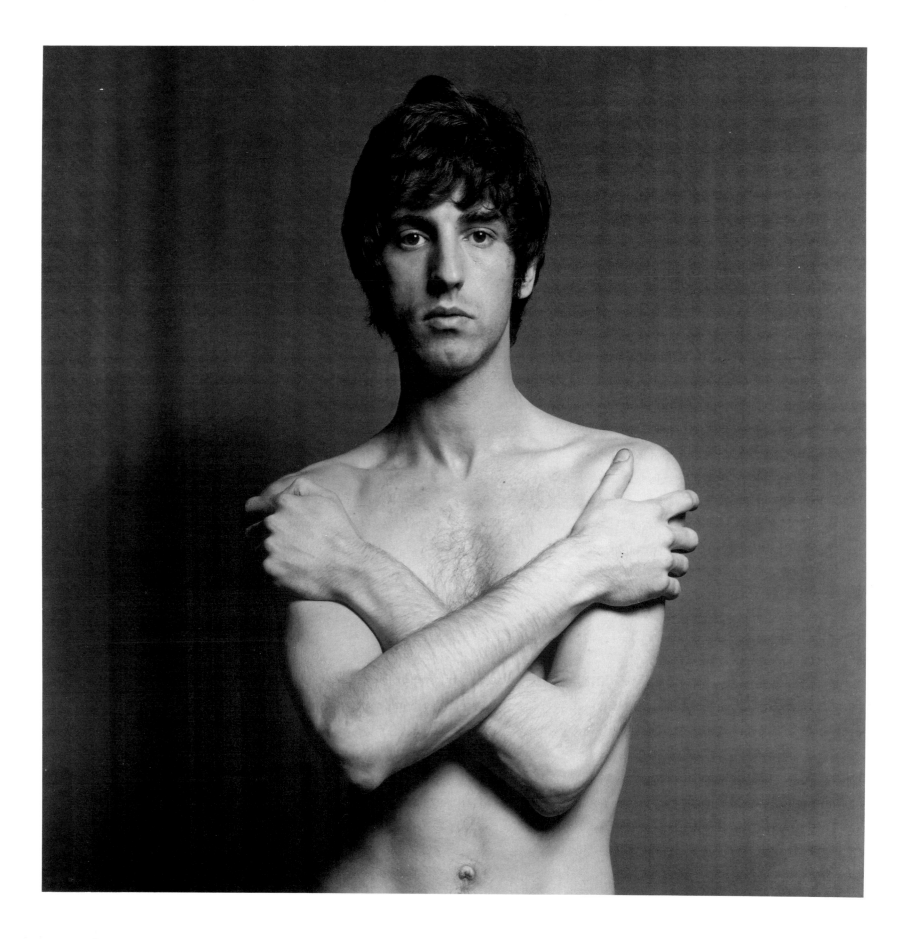

I N T R O D U C T I O N

Michael Cooper's photographs of the explosive early years of the Rolling Stones provide an intimacy and range that could only be captured by someone who, in addition to recording the scene, was also very much a part of what was happening. As with the Stones, Michael was enjoying himself and working continually—working not because it was Monday, nor because he was being commissioned (usually he wasn't), but because he truly possessed a burning passion to record and promote what he saw to be a period of unprecedented change. To that end, he looked upon his entire life as a photographic assignment. That, as Keith points out in his Foreword, is what is so amazing about these photographs.

Michael left Maidstone Art School to teach photography at Croydon College, then left the hallowed halls of Academia to work as a freelance photographer because, as he put it, while teaching he wasn't learning anything. Moving with his equally young bride and their newborn baby to a flat in Paulton Square, just off the King's Road, he was decidedly delighted to find himself slap-dab in the middle of the buzzing, fizzing pop culture bubbling through London at that time. He quickly met a wide range of artists, writers, aristocrats, and other shady characters, including, through the art dealer Robert Fraser, Anita Pallenberg and the Rolling Stones, together with a certain great American author, Terry (if indeed that is his name) Southern.

In addition to surviving on freelance assignments and a post as a junior staff photographer at Condé Nast, Michael was also

championing photography to Robert Fraser and other gallery owners, making the point—somewhat force-fully, by all accounts—that the results of photography could occasionally be viewed as something approaching Art. As Robert explained, "It might sound incredibly corny now, but remember that in those times Man Ray was practically unheard of, and here was this young guy not only talking about but showing how photography could be looked upon as an art form."

Toward the end of 1966, Robert set Michael up in his own studio at the Chelsea Manor studios in Flood Street, also just off the King's Road. Michael was finally free to apply his own creative ability to the people

and events happening all around him. It was an incredibly inspirational time. Real change seemed to be so possible, easily within reach; conventions could change, and the Stones were in a position to broadcast new attitudes and ideas and—who knows?—perhaps even bring a grain or two of common sense to the social structure people found them-selves forced to live by.

Michael formed a particularly strong friendship with Brian, Anita, and Keith, and through them created an incredible record of the dramatic developments and changes that influenced the band in a comparatively short period of time. His role was to provide, as he put it, "one involved person's view." Despite the backlash that set in so swiftly and with such venom against the hope, potential, and promise that had been such an inspiration for the few previous years, Michael continued to offer his view—not through any rose-tinted glasses, but simply to document both the good times and the terrible—"The triumphs, the tragedies, and the tears," as he put it. " 'No holds barred,' I think, is the expression."

The real disaster for Michael, however, was that by then, he'd also plummeted into a heroin addiction from which there appeared to be very little chance of recovery, and the tragedies began to eclipse everything else. Even in these circumstances he still enjoyed some wonderful times and persisted in taking fantastic photographs. But by 1972 the apparent evaporation of all the ideals he'd held so dear and the mounting problems and traumas in his personal life brought him to such a drastic point that suicide seemed the only way out of the deep depression into which he'd spiraled. One of the contributing factors to this despair was the seemingly complete lack of any wider appreciation for the work that he'd spent so much time, effort, care, and energy producing.

As several years ago this was still the case, I decided to collate Michael's collection and present these extraordinary images in the way that I felt they should be introduced.

I first met Michael when I was about thirteen and later worked as his assistant for a couple of years, so I knew, as Keith emphasizes in his Foreword, that Michael viewed his photographs as a particularly collaborative effort. It seemed natural to extend the theme of collaboration and have the text to the book take the form of captions, stories, and anecdotes by the people who appear in the photographs, talking about what's happening and the people in each of the

images. I talked to Keith about the idea and, again, it just seemed perfectly natural that he should provide the text. And if Anita and one of their (and Michael's) closest friends, tip-top Terry Southern, could also be involved, then we'd be sure of a text that's 110 percent authentic and would do justice to the character, quality, and range of the photographs.

In choosing the images for this book I selected a distillation that brings to light for the first time the full range of Michael's work with the Stones. He wrote of his work: "It is more than a record; these are available in vaster quantities and in much more detail from sources that are far beyond the resources of any individual—therein lies its wealth; it is a personal record. . . . History has thrown up many examples of periodic recording that was produced in the manner of primitive paintings, a sort of 'unconscious surrealism,' like a Busby Berkeley movie."

It seems to me that the engineering, attention to detail, artistry, and dedication that are so evident in the panoply of photographs that Michael "threw up" of the Stones are matched by the humor, honesty, and caliber of the memories pulled out of the air by Keith, Terry, and Anita. The combination offers a uniquely personal and original record of an era, seen through the lives of what's so often been dubbed the greatest rock 'n' roll band in the world.

—Perry Richardson
1992

CONTRIBUTORS

ADAM COOPER, a film-camera technician, is the son of Michael Cooper. He lives in Kingston-upon-Thames with his wife, Sylvia, and their baby, Emily.

MARIANNE FAITHFUL is a singer and an actress. She has starred in various successful film and stage productions. Her career as a singer began in 1964 with "As Tears Go By," composed by Mick Jagger and Keith Richards. Her relationship with Mick Jagger subsequently attracted the world's fascination. She currently lives in Ireland and has met with tremendous popular and critical acclaim in response to her latest world tours.

ANITA PALLENBERG, a contemporary of the Rolling Stones, has starred in films by directors such as Volker Schloendorf and in films that include *Barbarella, Candy, Night of the Generals*, and *Performance*. Brian Jones moved in with her in 1965. She then later lived with Keith Richards (with whom she has two children, Marlon and Angela) from 1967 to 1978. She currently lives in London and is completing a degree course in fashion design.

KEITH RICHARDS is a songwriter and the lead guitarist and a founding member of the Rolling Stones.

PERRY RICHARDSON was Michael Cooper's assistant for two years from the age of seventeen. He is currently a publishing director and musician. He lives in Devon, England, with his wife, Elen, and their children, Edward and Jamie.

TERRY SOUTHERN is the author of several novels, including *The Magic Christian, Flash and Filigree, Blue Movie*, and, most recently, *Texas Summer*. Coauthor of *Candy*, he is also a reknowned screenwriter whose work includes such movie classics as *Dr. Strangelove, Easy Rider, The Loved One*, and *Barbarella*. A close friend of Keith Richards for more than twenty-five years, he currently lives with Gail Gerber in Connecticut and New York.

THE EARLY STONES

KEITH:

this is the "Too Many Hands" photo. I've actually gone to the trouble of counting all the hands. Yes. Well, that's the kind of thing Michael is inclined to do, ten people and the eleventh hand there. I'm trying to get the hand but I can't. I don't know . . . Michael . . .

TERRY:

Well, we know it isn't your hand because of the . . .

KEITH:

Yeah . . . I'm sure these are all the band's hands. This totally escaped me at the time and I have never noticed it before, but this is a typical Michael's chick hand. It comes back from the grave, this one. Obviously he had someone behind . . . Who could it be? My only thought is that when Michael did a photo session like this, he'd always have an assistant, you know—it could be anybody. Is it a chick's hand—the nails are very well manicured, aren't they? I wonder who can tell us . . . maybe we should ask Charlie—he always had an eye for the young female hand. No, it's too big for a woman's hand; it's also manicured differently, but at the same time it's a very nice hand, not a guitar player's hand. Well, this is one of the things Michael left us to figure out—a Laurel and Hardy sort of thing.

3

KEITH:

nita's flat in Courtfield Road—and there's my note. Couldn't find any paper so I wrote it on the wall—"Call you tomorrow." . . .

TERRY:

And doubtless did so . . . Is this where you learned to write songs?

KEITH:

Yes, a crash course, you might say.

TERRY:

When Andrew Oldham locked the two of you in the kitchen, that was a bit drastic, wasn't it?

KEITH:

It turned out to be a good move. We'd been playing famous old black American jazz/blues tunes. "You can't survive playing other people's music," he said, and he somehow tricked us into the kitchen, locked the door, and said, "Now, stay there until you've written a song." Maybe it was just to humor him, but we did stay, started fooling around and wrote something—something pretty awful probably, but good enough to get us out of the kitchen. Actually it was "As Tears Go By"—very un-Stonelike—but we persuaded Marianne Faithful to record it, and a couple of weeks later it was in the Top Ten. That's when Mick and I looked at each other and said, "Well, maybe we can write songs."

ANITA:

It was just excitement for me really.
Even though it was my flat in Courtfield
Road, I'd go off and leave 'em there.
Actually I'd be quite envious of them
really, because there I was making films,
which is great, but I always had this
problem with authority and there were
all of these producers, all of these people, and I had to deal with it all, whereas
from what I'd seen of how the Stones
operate, their attitude was, "Oh, fuck
'em all!" and they totally got away with
it. I think Andrew was the most outrageous of them all—I mean, oh God, he
could be so cutting and everything, real
arrogant—but then the whole band was
the same. They were very close, very
young and they didn't give a damn. They
were just doing what they did.

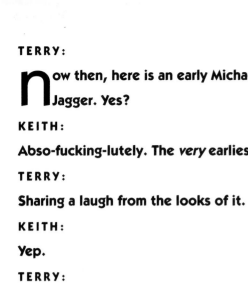

TERRY:

now then, here is an early Michael Cooper pic of you and young Jagger. Yes?

KEITH:

Abso-fucking-lutely. The *very* earliest, I'd say.

TERRY:

Sharing a laugh from the looks of it.

KEITH:

Yep.

TERRY:

I don't suppose you can recall the nature of your mirth at that point in time?

KEITH:

Oh, I dunno, something to do with Alienation and Despair, I shouldn't wonder . . . ha-ha.

TERRY:

now this is a rather striking picture—you and Brian near water's
edge at the early hour. Just what body
of water is this, if I may ask?

KEITH:

Well, let's see . . . I'm going to say . . .
Hyde Park Serpentine.

TERRY:

Some have said this picture represents a
deeply private moment. Not necessarily
one of bonding mind, but deeply
private.

KEITH:

Deciding who's going to drown whom,
no doubt. You'll note that Michael is
more focused on the water than on
either of us. He often considered us
peripheral in his shots.

Hyde Park Serpentine, at the early
hour . . .

KEITH:

Probably coming from Robert Fraser's, on
our way to Brian's pad, with Michael in
tow.

TERRY:

Having spent the night in a right rave-up,
I warrant.

KEITH:

And now seeking refuge.

TERRY:

As in "Gimme Shelter"? . . .

KEITH:

Right. Looking for meaning . . . looking
for a sign . . .

ANITA:

This is a very sweet shot. When I was living with Brian in the really early days, there'd always be fans outside the house in Elm Park Mews, and they'd say, "Can we come in and have a cup of tea?" and I'd say, "Yeah, yeah—come on." And so then they'd wash up—then they'd say, "Can we make Brian's bed?" and so I'd say, "Yeah, o.k., do it." So they were quite useful! Later it became just tarts and all of that, but these were just sweet, very innocent little girls.

Brian and I always kept our clothes all together. He was always keen on going out to the shops, trying everything on, putting it all together. He loved it—and he definitely had it—the knack for doing it—and by then he'd given up on his white trousers, become much more sophisticated, really! He always had this thing about cutting his hair—it was always such a big scene to cut his hair. He had to have three mirrors, and he'd sit there and I'd be so terrified, because I usually cut his hair, and it was like "Oh God!"; it was a nightmare for me—tiny little bits at a time . . . incredible—and he'd get so pissed off and angry; I mean, it was terrible because he was also very vain, you know—very, very vain.

In the early days he was too busy whizzing around, booking the dates, getting it all together, to write any songs, but from a little bit later onwards from what I remember, Brian was writing songs constantly. The only thing is that he didn't have the confidence and he just erased them—he'd just screw 'em up, get rid of them—chuck 'em in the fire. And then I think that Andrew just ignored him or whatever—never encouraged him but just got Mick and Keith to start writing songs.

KEITH:

brian on cello at Olympic Studios, recording "Ruby Tuesday," even though he didn't end up playing cello. Bill and I played it. It took two of us to play it. We found out if you're not actually a cello player it takes at least two guys to play the thing.

TERRY:

Could cause a spot of bother in the musicians' union, yes?

KEITH:

Yeah, if this gets into print, we'll probably get something in the post. Infractions of the rules, paragraph 7-2-39, et cetera.

ANITA:

Michael and Jane Rainey were part of that aristocratic scene, but with no airs and graces. Jane was just a positively raving person—I met her before I met the Stones . . . and Christopher Gibbs, Marc Palmer, Tara Browne. I remember I was really shocked at this kind of very English world. For instance, I went once to Jane's house for tea and her mother was there with this other girl, a friend of the family who was on probation for stealing. And she had this probation officer sitting there with her, and she was going, "Oh fuck off—shut it!" I was totally shocked at this young girl treating this older woman in that way, and then I found out it was actually her probation officer! So these girls were all really pretty tough chicks—but then they were out to have loads of fun as well. And Jane—I mean, I love her still to this day; she's one of my heroines really . . . and Michael was just so wonderful and so handsome—I think everybody I knew had a crush on him in those days—Robert, Chrissie, we all had a crush on him.

Once with the Stones—it was the Ad Lib, one of those clubs—everybody was just on these benches, eyeing each other. Keith was going, "What the fucking hell do these guys want?" and they were all going "Chat, chat, chat, chat, chat, chat," all frivolous and everything, and Keith was saying, "Fucking tarts, assholes, cunts!" But Brian . . . if someone liked Brian, then he liked them as well. If somebody'd say, "Oh, Brian, you're great," he'd just go "Ohhh" and completely melt. So for a while, this whole scene became an outlet for him, to kind of find his own territory aside from the Stones. The way I saw it, Mick and Keith pretty quickly realized that those people all had something that the Stones wanted, and the Stones had what all of these kind of decadent aristocrats wanted—all these girls and that kind of action and singing and playing music. It seemed to them so romantic at the time, and so it kind of fell together— they both had what the other one wanted—so it was very compatible because of that and quite exciting really, and very nice, too. And it was a crash course in good manners for the Stones as well. Not that they became "well behaved" or anything like that—I mean, they were still outrageous—but they could see that there was a different background, and some of the courtesies, for instance, were actually rather charming. It also actually made the Stones wiser much more quickly.

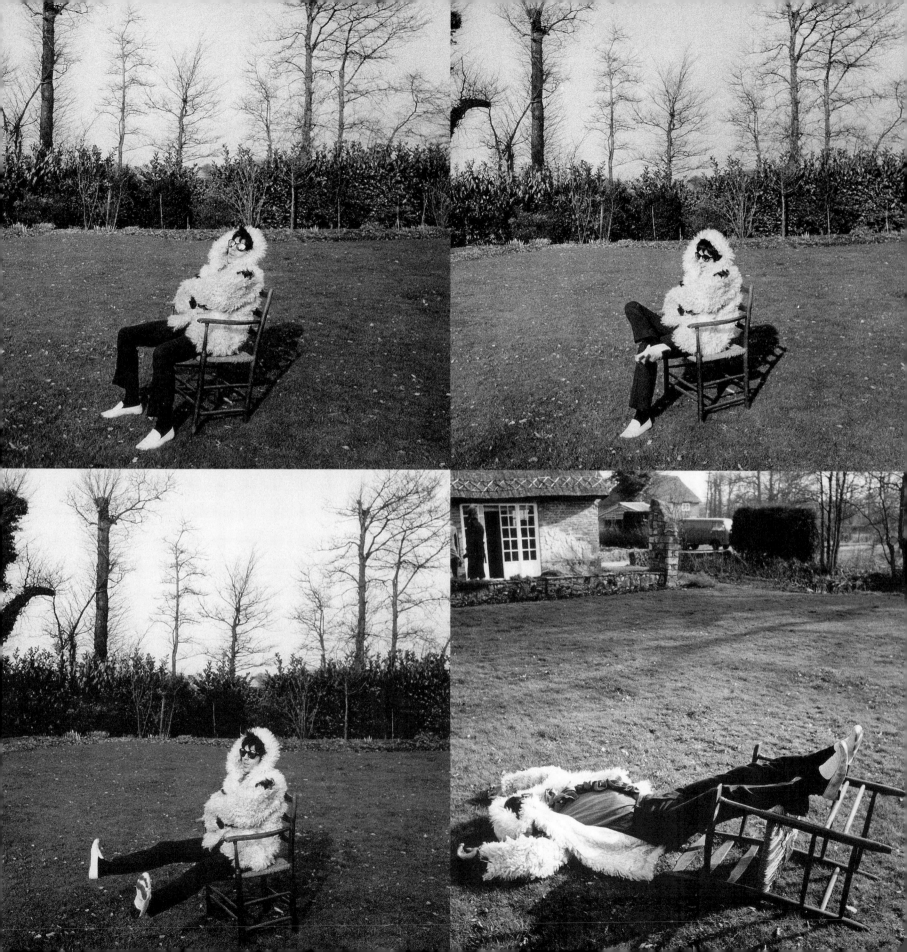

KEITH:

ahh, Redlands [Keith and Anita's house in Sussex]. This was just after the bust.

TERRY:

Any recollection of that as it came down?

KEITH:

Public record. We had all turned in after an early supper and a bit of a singalong by the cozy hearth. Then, well into the night, there was this great row and bloody din below stairs—which proved to be the constabulary and that lot, turning the premises upside down in search of illicit substances.

TERRY:

I trust they didn't try any roughhouse.

KEITH:

No, thankfully we were spared their usual tactics.

TERRY:

Because of the women being present?

KEITH:

That may have helped.

ANITA:

I was working pretty continually throughout this whole period—modeling, filming . . . Brian got involved in the music for one of my films, and that was another major number. To a certain extent, though, that was a breakthrough, because Jimmy Page and Brian did the music for that film, which was presented in Cannes. That was the first time that had happened—rock stars writing the sound track for a movie. So I'd been in Germany doing the film. I'd just got back and Brian, who was supposed to have finished the music, had finally been given a deadline. Everyone had gone down to Redlands, so we said we'd just finish the music, then join them. Then, when we called up, Keith said, "Don't bother coming, because

they've just busted us." It was as drastic as that. Then they busted Brian in London. But by then there was already an outrage in reaction to the busts. I think that basically what they wanted to do was make an example to the youth— they hoped that it would scare the people—but it certainly didn't work. I mean, Keith just found it extraordinary—the charge and that the reaction to it came so quickly, on such a scale. I remember the charge against Keith—turning out to be that he was allowing his place to be used for people to be taking drugs in— seemed so ridiculous. And that charge is still on the books. But the way we reacted was just to leave, to go to Morocco—get away, go somewhere where it's legal.

28

KEITH:

Iike a picture from a dream isn't it?
Is that copper by Marianne Pete
Townsend?!

KEITH:

the arresting officers—complete with
file—took away all our incense and
left most of the drugs.

KEITH:

Satanic Majesties! Michael got you up to some amazing things. I mean, here we're making our own set for the fucking album cover—"Got the glue?" "Can I have that saw when you've finished with it?"

KEITH:

handicrafts for two or three days, you know—kept popping out and buying things when we ran out. Bits of styrofoam and God knows what. Millions of bits of sequins, rhinestones, and beads!

MARIANNE:

In Tangiers Mick and I would stay at Sidi Mamoun, Paul and Taleedtha Getty's palace. We went there quite a lot, but this was the first time—I think straight after that bust. I always think that we went there because Mick would enjoy it much more going to stay in a beautiful palace with servants and food and everything laid on rather than paying out a fortune for some hotel somewhere.

Mick liked that scene, you know, High Society, or he thought it was. I mean, we went once for Christmas to the Earl of Warwick's house and it was beautiful and there were footmen behind every chair and I took a couple of mandys and, er, passed out in the soup, which is not . . . well, depends on your attitude really, but Mick was so humiliated, but *so* humiliated by this—he had to carry me upstairs and put me to bed—and this just wasn't done. I'm not saying I'm terribly proud of myself, and I wasn't doing it just because it was Warwick Castle—you know, I just happened to feel like it.

KEITH:

So this is on the getaway from Marra-kesh when I took her away from Beasty Brian.

TERRY:

Don't forget you took half the records and half the dope.

KEITH:

Well, they were mine!

TERRY:

No, I thought it was very considerate to leave half—I mean, you could have taken everything.

KEITH:

Yeah, well I had a one-track mind at the time. Thought, "Here, I'll leave you something."

ANITA:

brian was suffering badly at this point—severe fits of paranoia. Started taking his clothes off on the street in Morocco—we'd have to hustle him into doorways, somehow get him back to the hotel.

But he'd also become intrigued and very excited about the rhythm and music of Jujuku, the tribe he'd met through Brion Gysin, who was a very good influence on him. I'd already made my decision about him before this trip to Africa—I'd already been enchanted and swept up by Keith. Brian knew that and so all in all decided to stay on in Tangiers at Brion Gysin's.

ANITA:

this was at Kevin Brownjohn's studios. He did the titles for films—*Goldfinger, The Woman Painted in Gold*—all kinds of stuff. Did the titles for *Night of the Generals* with me, too. Also, he did that cover with the cake for the Stones—*Let It Bleed.*

TERRY:

I was wondering if I could interest you in a stroll down Memory Lane regarding some of your more colorful drug busts?

KEITH:

Wot?

TERRY:

When you think back on it, does any one of them emerge as a sort of favorite?

KEITH:

Not bloody likely.

TERRY:

I was thinking of the so-called "Canadian Caper." What was that all about?

KEITH:

Oh, well, that was all a bit of a mix-up, really. All blown out of proportion by a lot of silly journalists, if you see what I mean.

TERRY:

I gather you don't care to talk about it.

KEITH:

Well, it's all over now, isn't it? It's all in the past.

TERRY:

And you don't like talking about the past, is that it?

KEITH:

Oh, I don't *mind* talking about the past, except that it's sort of pointless, isn't it?

. . . like old rubbish. I guess I'm a bit of an existentialist in some respects—like the past being nothing but old rubbish, and all that . . .

TERRY:

Yes . . . well, what actually happened then? I mean, just how did it come down?

KEITH:

Well, it was really quite simple. We were coming into Canada by car, at about three in the morning, my old lady at the wheel, and me getting a bit of kip in the back seat——

I'm sorry, I'm referring to the Toronto Airport "incident"—wasn't that where it happened?

KEITH:

No, no, no, that was pure rubbish, just journalistic claptrap—*News of the World* and that lot—trying to make it all sound very la-di-da and *romantic* . . . you know, "last plane out of Lisbon," that sort of thing. I actually *read* some of that clap-trap—all rubbish. They had *no idea* what really happened. Airport indeed! What bloody rubbish!

TERRY:

Well, what did in fact happen?

KEITH:

Yes . . . well, like I say, we were just crossing into Canada—big Bentley, very comfy—especially for me, having a rest in the back seat . . . then we *stops*—it's Border Time . . . Checkpoint Charlie Time—you know the scene: "Bla-bla this, bla-bla that." "What's all this lot?" "What's all that lot?" Bloody bore. Any-way, nothing is happening except that Anita is rooting about in her purse for something—license, registration, that sort of thing—and I'm, like I say, having a kip on the back seat. But I'm not really *asleep*, you dig, just on the noddy-like, so I take a *look*—not a *big* look, mind, just a bit of the old peeka-roo—to see what's coming down. And there's this

→

great bloody harness-bull, Mountie style, sort of leaning over, peering into the car, flashing his torch about, in what *could've* been a most disturbing fashion, except for me being so fatigued and oblivious-like, having my rest—and a well-deserved one it was, if I may say—so I don't stir, even though he put a bloody light full in my face at one point. But meanwhile I'm clocking his act, squinty style, and as far as he knows I'm heavily into the kip copping some *z*'s, even audibly so, if memory serves—and Anita still fishing around in the bag for the license . . . and that's when he did it: He reached out and, very deliberate-like, picked something off her shoulder—a bit of lint, or *dandruff* maybe—I don't think she *has* dandruff actually, *never* had dandruff, but *he* thought it was dandruff . . . So he picks it up, between thumb and finger, and then straightaway—are you ready for this?—he *pops it into his gullet!* And I'm lying in the back seat, watching this come down, and I think to myself, "Well now, here's as odd a bit of the old perversion as I've seen in quite a while!" And I'm wondering if I can believe my eyes, when lo and behold, he does it again. And this time the old lady notices it as well—not that he's having a nosh on her dandruff, mind, *that* would've freaked her

right out—but just that he's *touching* her on the shoulder, tapping-like, and she gives him a straight look and says: "What is it? What are you doing?" "Just doing my duty, miss," he says, sounding all creepy-crawly. And that's when a certain yours truly leaped into the breach, so to speak. "*Oh?*" I said, a bit sharp and sarky, "and what *duty* might it be that compels you to have a nosh on me missus' dandruff!?"

"Eh?" he said, wheeling about—"Wot? Wot?"—surprised he was at my coming up on him so sudden, and him confronted, as it were, with his own gross weirdness. Then his mate comes over. "What's up, partner?" he says. "I can tell you what's up," I says, getting more indignant. "Your so-called partner is a *bloody sex maniac,*" I said. "A right raver he is! Trying to nosh me missus' dandruff! Bloody gross, I call it!" Then of course *she* has to pipe up: "I do *not* have dandruff!" "Don't *you* start in," I say. "That's hardly the bloody point"—and here I've got my hands full with *this* pair of weirdies. But the twisted copper—maniac preeve that he was—remained un-bloody-fazed. I mean, he was trapped, you see, and there was no place for him to go but *straight ahead.* "Ay," he says, all tersed up, right out of bloody "Z Squad," "looks like we've got a nasty one this time—and maybe a *big* one as well." Then he actually makes out that he's picking another bit off her shoulder. "Flake," he says, then tastes it—probably a part of his kick—know what I mean?—doing it in front of people—"*Peruvian* flake, if my guess is any good, and probably more where this came from! Call H.Q. *we're taking 'em in!*"

Well, by now I'm ready to punch him out. "You swine!" I shout, falling right into the old stereotype of the raving rocker. "I'm not taking a fall for *your* weirdo act!"

Well . . . I was wrong, and the rest, as Lord Balfour—I think it was Lord Balfour—said, is history.

But it all worked out in the end, so I'm now quite prepared to raise a glass of the great J.D.—to Canadian jurisprudence, et cetera, et cetera.

KEITH:

ndrew learned record producing at the same time we did. The only reason he's sitting there is because we were on the other side playing the stuff. I mean, Andrew knew nothing about recording except what he thought he wanted to hear, which may be the purest way of producing because he is not going to turn to the engineer and say, "Wait a minute. I want more bla-bla-bla." It must be maddening when somebody does that. But in those days it didn't matter because it was all in bloody mono. It was like you were going for a certain sound and a lot of the time Andrew was right. I mean, he was trying to make records that *he* wanted to listen to and so were we, and most of the time he was right with all his enthusiasm and so on. And he was quick to learn. I mean, when he found out how to do something that worked with the Stones, he didn't forget it. He was very resourceful.

But we started to learn more than Andrew did, and all of a sudden Mick and I figured that possibly we had more of an idea what this band could do than Andrew did. Jack Nitzsche, for instance, would come in and help us get just the sound we wanted.

Andrew just wanted hit records; we wanted great ones. But Andrew should get a lot of credit. He was very smart. He got us one of the best engineers around, Glyn Johns.

Actually, it was Johns who recorded our very first session even before Andrew was involved with us, and Andrew, as I say, was no dummy, and he would always make sure that he had the best people around him.

⇥

TERRY:

And good equipment?

KEITH:

Well, equipment is not really where it's at. I mean, a lot of that stuff we were listening to earlier [some great old Jimmy Witherspoon records] was cut on two-track Grundig. It's to do with the performance, not what you pick it up on. Whatever is available. Everything becomes more and more toy-town as far as technology goes. You see, the thing with recording is that it's just duplication. The thing is that when you're making records, it's impossible to be in two places at the same time. I mean, you do the thing and you think it's good, and then you have to come in and listen to the playback and find out whether they've really caught what's going on out there. And if they haven't, why not? Because that means you're going to have to do it again. Or does it mean it's actually on the tape and that it will take some manipulation through one of these levers and knobs to find it? Is it really on the tape or isn't it? That's the freaky part: "That's the tape." "That's not the tape."

TERRY:

So when you go into a recording session, you're not entirely sure what's going to happen . . .

KEITH:

You can never know for sure. You've got to know what you're going in for before you cut the first thing. If you cut a rhythm track with the idea of overlaying it, then it has to be cut in a certain way. You need your rhythm section really crisp and tight, and the bass and drums should be perfect, so there's no problem about working on top of it. It can't have any soft edges.

TERRY:

So you do go in with certain assumptions.

KEITH:

Yeah . . . well, it depends what song it is. You are going to go in there with this particular song—

TERRY:

Let's say "Brown Sugar."

KEITH:

We are going to have no overdubs on this, we are just going to cut the performance. Everybody is going to go in there and play it, and we're going to cut it and that's it.

TERRY:

No sweetening required . . .

KEITH:

No sweetening, no fairy dust. We go in and get a performance. That's how this record should be made. You may have another song and want to play guitars over it. Then you would cut the rhythm section very, very precisely. It would have to be perfect, so you could play over the top of it several times and you're not going to worry about any glitches, and free-form time, et cetera, so that you keep going over and over and it still sounds ethical.

KEITH:

U.S. Immigration control—they'd pulled us off the plane for some "extra interrogation." "Just trying to grease my way into your country, your worship"—making all the right moves! Ahh, I don't know . . . the carelessness of youth!

In fact, they wouldn't give me a proper entry visa to the States for ages. Then I got busted in Canada, with this monstro charge sheet. But on the tour we'd been doing there I'd noticed this one very sweet-looking, pretty young girl who was obviously blind, right up by the front of the stage at our first gig. Next show,

however many hundreds of miles away, there she was again, right up at the front of the stage. So I remember thinking, "Well, it's pretty obvious she's out to follow the tour," but I mean how's she going to get from place to place . . . and also it can get decidedly rough, right up there at the front of those gigs. So I asked the roadies to look after her— gave them some money to give to her, made sure she could get from gig to gig, ride with the trucks if she wanted to. So anyhow, then we get busted—badly— and it turns out that this little girl knows or is related to the judge who's trying the case. So totally unbeknownst to me, she ups and goes along to see this judge at his home, explains this story of how I've looked out for her and all that, and the upshot is that he passes a ruling that as the major payment for the offence we have to play a free concert at this blind school in Vermont. So then on top of that, because this "sentence" is a legal edict, I also get the entry visa I've been trying so long to get ahold of—I mean, it is also true that in some ways no coun- try likes to bust the Stones—bad PR basically—so there might've been a little bit of that going on, too, but I doubt it in this case quite honestly. Ninety per- cent of it at least, I'd say, was due to the little blind girl who swung it so that getting busted in Canada got me my entry visa into the States.

ANITA:

On their first tour of America I went out to meet them in Dallas, if I remember—paid my own ticket, met up, had dinner with the roadies, and then went back to the hotel—and it was all like that then, not organized. None of those "passes" or any of that shit. Those were days when if they had a hotel room they'd wreck it, completely, on the adrenaline they had when they came off stage. I mean, I've never experienced it but I guess that's what it must have been—rather than make a fool of your-self in a club or something, just have these really wild parties back at the hotel. These shots look pretty normal. I guess they were taken before the gig.

On the second tour to America, in-stead of hotels like Howard Johnson's, it'd be the Beverly Wilshire, the Bel-Air—a whole lot better. Didn't stop us wreck-ing 'em though!

But it was the girls, really, who were shocking the hotel people. I mean, they'd never seen anything like it. I re-member staying in hotels with Brian and there'd be all this stuff going on outside in the corridor, and the moment we got out of bed there were camera flashes

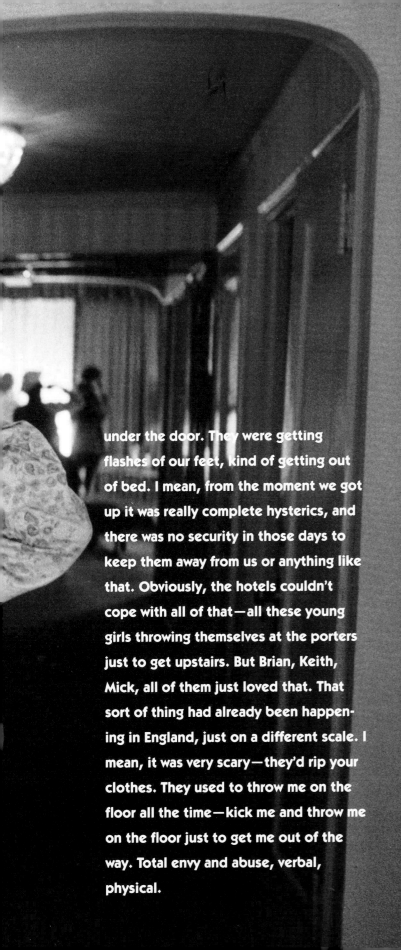

under the door. They were getting flashes of our feet, kind of getting out of bed. I mean, from the moment we got up it was really complete hysterics, and there was no security in those days to keep them away from us or anything like that. Obviously, the hotels couldn't cope with all of that—all these young girls throwing themselves at the porters just to get upstairs. But Brian, Keith, Mick, all of them just loved that. That sort of thing had already been happening in England, just on a different scale. I mean, it was very scary—they'd rip your clothes. They used to throw me on the floor all the time—kick me and throw me on the floor just to get me out of the way. Total envy and abuse, verbal, physical.

TERRY:

morning after the Redlands bust is what I make of this shot.

KEITH:

So it would appear.

TERRY:

I can just make out the headline:

> NAKED GIRL AT
>
> STONES PARTY

And that girl was, correct me if I am wrong, a certain Ms. M. Faithful.

KEITH:

Well, I believe it's a matter of, how do you say, public record. Actually she was covered with a fur coat.

TERRY:

She may have flashed. Flashed the coppers.

KEITH:

Marianne? Not bloody likely.

TERRY:

Flashed the coppers to craze them, you see. She's fabulously endowed by all accounts.

KEITH:

But it wouldn't be like Marianne to flash the coppers, or anyone else for that matter. Too much class. In fact, I think she had gone to bed and had the coat over her.

TERRY:

As a simple coverlet.

KEITH:

Exactly.

71

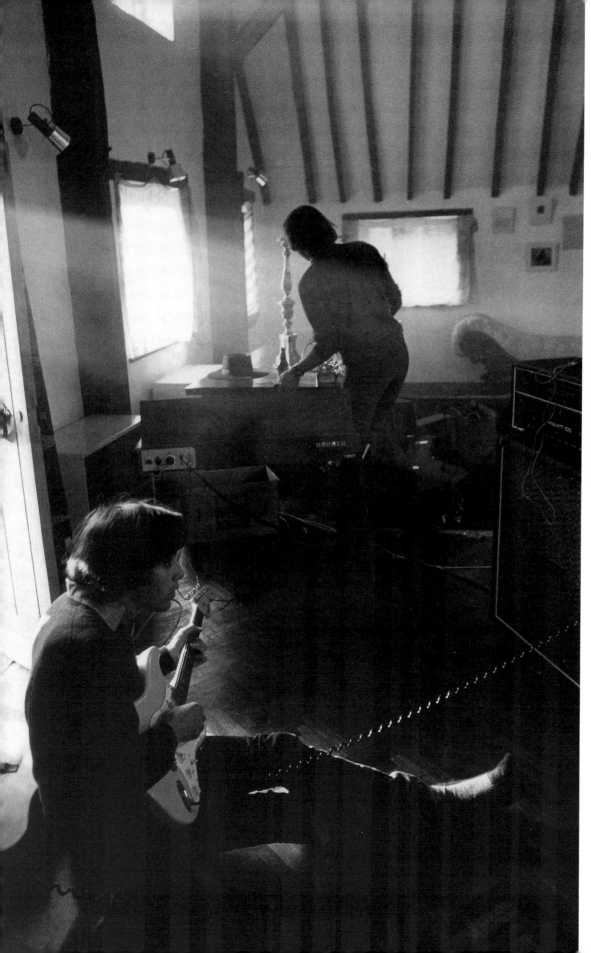

KEITH:

ry Cooder visiting the Fifth Dimension. That was my cottage! Down-
stairs in part of it we knocked three
rooms into one and called it the Fifth
Dimension. It was great, and mostly
everyone used to come over there.
"C'mon, everybody over to Keith's!"

ANITA:

Yeah, Ry Cooder came down to visit for the weekend. He was just passed out, as I remember, on the couch. Then he'd just get up and play. He was a very quiet person, but then I was probably as passed out as he was—so it's difficult to remember any meaningful things that might have been exchanged!

KEITH:

his is a perfect picture of Ian Stewart at the piano. It sort of personifies the very first time that we really put the band together, the Rolling Stones, before we had a name, and I went to this pad where we were rehearsing, just off Wardour Street. I went upstairs, and Stu was there, looking just about like that, sitting at the piano. Many years later, after he died, I was talking to Charlie about it and said that in a way I was still working for Stu and that it was like it was his band—he had been so strong—and no matter what went down, he never

really left the band except in the most superficial way of not being on the album cover photographs because he didn't look the part. But in other respects, he was always with us, and he did still play with us, and it was him we looked to—not so much for approval, but to be sure there wasn't his disapproval. If there was something he didn't like or if we were trying to do something you didn't understand, we would have to have a very long talk with Stu and get it sorted out as to why this particular song was not something we should do, because, as he sometimes put it, we

would be "barking up the wrong tree with that load of fucking Chinese crap." Stu was a master at turning a phrase like that, and he enjoyed taking the piss out of us. "You like to think of yourselves as blues musicians," he would say, "but you just prance around like screaming little nance boys." Or he could do it with an eyebrow or a shrug—devastate you. But then, there was the other side of the coin when you'd be wondering, "Is this swinging? Or am I just kidding myself?" and you'd turn around and Stu would be beaming from ear to ear, and you'd know it was fine.

IAN STEWART:

Me, I like black men's music and scuba diving. The only music they've done that I really didn't like was some of that Satanic Majesties stuff, bits of which still just leave me stone cold.

I suppose you could say that there was a time when people thought they had to be junkies to hang around with the Stones, but Keith certainly never made drugs a condition. That was always something he did for his own reasons . . . never insisted that anyone else should do it. In fact, quite the opposite in many

cases. And Mick's somebody who's just a bit of a dabbler, really. I don't think he was ever actually hooked on anything is what I mean. I'm quite sure he's tried it all and taken what he wants and left the rest alone. Brian was, in my view, someone who never should have taken drugs—it just made him worse. He was someone who could be taken quite easily anyway by the sort of leech that wanted to sponge off him. Whereas Keith wasn't quite so easy to get taken.

There was a time—I'm talking now basically about Brian and Keith—when

they had a tight little crew of friends who all seemed to be trying to outdo themselves with how many drugs they could take—had little competitions to see who could take the most. I could never see it—I've never seen the need for it—and Bill's never seen the need for it, nor has Charlie, really. Charlie could always be around those guys and sort of always enjoy their company, but he could always do it without getting out of it on drugs. I never could, you know—couldn't stand the smoke!

77

KEITH:

t hat's a good picture of Andrew. Andrew Oldham was this extraordinary young man—younger than any of us— who loved music but had a very irreverent attitude toward the music industry in general and the record business in particular. He also had a flair for PR, which he had previously done for the Beatles. I suppose it was his idea really to make us into something like the opposite of the Beatles—so that to the extent they looked all clean-cut and good, we would look scruffy and evil. For instance, I think it was Andrew who started the newspaper slogan: "The Band That Children Love and Parents Hate," and that other bit of rubbish: "Would You Let Your Daughter Marry a Rolling Stone?"

ANITA:

Marianne met the Stones through Andrew. Through John—I think she was already married to John [Dunbar] by then, and they had their baby, Nicholas. She was very coy and very straight—kind of like a pearl on velvet—Laura Ashley kind of stuff. And then, of course, she ended up with Mick and all of that.

I always had great admiration for her. I always found it amazing how on "As Tears Go By," for instance, her voice kind of tremeloed . . . it was like vibrato. I was always completely fascinated by her. She always looked like such a fragile little girl, and then at the same time she was also very tough. I mean, she left John—left the whole thing behind and then started to go out with Mick and then started to become quite ruthless, actually, and then she changed all her outfits. I remember her once saying to me when she was going with Mick that she wanted me to take her to buy some clothes. Well, she bought a chandelier and four or six stags—you know, the heads with horns—and God knows what else. So as I say, I was always just sort of fascinated by this kind of over-the-top person.

TERRY:

brian looks like a sort of fun guy in this picture, doesn't he?

KEITH:

The rotten bastard. Have you noticed he's actually reading a magazine there? This is probably a train magazine.

TERRY:

A train-buff mag?

KEITH:

He and Stu were both avid steam-train freaks.

TERRY:

I don't believe that's generally known.

KEITH:

Well, you have to understand that London had some of the greatest marshalling yards in the kingdom. Even when we were on the road with Stu and Brian, they'd forever be up on some bridge somewhere watching the last few locomotives, trying to spot the *Golden Arrow* or *Flying Scotsman*.

TERRY:

Someone said you have written the sound track of your generation. What do you think?

KEITH:

Very complimentary, I'm sure.

What I can say is that when I play that first riff in "Jumping Jack Flash," something happens in my stomach—a feeling of tremendous exhilaration, an amazing superhuman feeling. An *explosion* is the best way to describe it. You just jump on that riff, and *it plays you*. It's the one feeling I would say approaches the state of nirvana.

My first experience relating to the Rolling Stones was in London, in 1963, when I met Michael Cooper in Duke Street, outside Robert Fraser's art gallery at number 69. We were both looking for Robert. It was a gray winter afternoon, and the gallery was closed.

"What's the time, then?" Michael asked. I told him it was about four.

"Oh well then," he said, sounding like someone out of Lewis Carroll, "if that's the case, he's most likely popped over to his mum's for tea."

"Yes, of course," I said, trying to get into his Mad Hatter mode, "that's sure to be it."

"Yes, he'll not be back today," he went on, but when he noticed my disappointment, he beamed, and added: "We can wait for him at the flat."

His expression "the flat" could not have been more apt for the establishment at 120 Mount Street. From 1960 until his death in 1972, Robert Fraser's flat in Mount Street was a veritable mecca for the movers and groovers of the '60s scene. Calling it "the flat" was also an indication of the Damon/Pythias tightness of Michael and Robert—an indication hallmarked in spades, so to speak, when Michael produced his own latch-key and let us in.

"It seems we're not alone," he noted as we got into the lift and heard the muted but wafting blast of Little Richard's "Good Golly Miss Molly" from three floors above.

"It's probably Brian's new bird," he said. "She seems to be staying here now."

Michael had this extraordinary habit of assuming you knew people you'd never met, and then somehow making you believe you did know them quite well.

"Anita, she's called," he went on. "She's really quite an ultra."

The most voguish superlative in London at the moment was the word *fab*. In some circles *ultra* was used to augment it; so that a girl of supreme beauty might be referred to as "an ultra fab." To use the word *ultra* by itself, however, in the nominative case—as Michael had done, saying, "She's quite an *ultra*"—was an example of the creative speech heard in the streets of London at the time. It was also, as I saw when she opened the door, most appropriate in the case of Anita Pallenberg—a German model/actress with an electrifying Kurt Weill/von Stroheim aura. Although she was only nineteen or twenty at the time, she bore a mesmerizing resemblance to the celebrated international beauty Valli, of *The Third Man* fame.

It was in Munich after a concert that she managed—without great difficulty, one may assume—to get backstage and meet the boys. Keith recalls the historic occasion: "We were falling all over ourselves, because of her drop-dead beauty, trying to persuade her to play a bit of the old 'Hide-the-knockwurst,' but it was Brian she fancied, and Brian who copped her." He laughed. "Don't forget, he was the leader of the band."

It was true, of course, that it was Brian's band; it was Brian who put it together, and Brian who named it. He was the leader, both musically and in the libidos of his femme rock-fans. And it is interesting, not to mention superbly ironic, that Brian's "vulnerability" was and is invariably cited as the reason for his deadly attractiveness to women, when he proved to be a fervent misogynist and notorious brutalizer of women.

Naturally, this did not appear to be the case during those halcyon days when Anita was being squired about on the veloured arm of Brian's Edwardian jacket, or tooling around Old Smoke in his fab white Rolls. Later she would recount to me the details of their cyclonic courtship. It seems that during the finale of the Stones' Hamburg concert, the ever sensitive Brian suffered a slight—real or imaginary— from Mick and Keith, regarding his performance.

"When I got backstage," she recalled, "I went straight to Brian, because he was the one I fancied. I tapped him on the shoulder and had a big smile ready for him when he turned around." She laughed as she remembered the scene. "I could hardly believe it, but he was on the verge of tears, and for a weird moment I thought it was somehow my fault! 'Well,' I said to myself, 'we're off to a rather shaky start!' " She soon learned, of course, that the cause for Brian's disquiet was less ethereal. It was, in fact, merely a part of the running torment Mick and Keith subjected him to, onstage and off. "Getting Brian's goat, we call it," Keith once told me.

According to Anita, Brian was so upset on the occasion of their first meeting that he was "quite beyond sex." His eyes brimming with tears, he begged her to spend the night with him. "It wasn't a sex thing," Anita insisted. "He just wanted someone to hold him. He cried all night."

The next day apparently found him in better spirits, but still in dire need of her companionship. He begged her to accompany him and the band on the rest of the German tour, and it is interesting to speculate to what extent such a surprise guest would have freaked Mick Jagger and Keith Richards. Anita now says she probably *would* have gone with him if she hadn't had several important fashion bookings in another direction. But she immediately called her agency in Berlin and told them to book her some work in London.

And now she was indeed on the London scene, her wit and beauty destined to grace many a smart salon and disco in days to come—as well as to shape the future of the Stones themselves.

The sensational thing about Brian and Anita—the thing that caused the sophistos at Annabel's and Scott's Piccadilly to gawk like bumpkins—was not just the bewitching beauty of the couple, but their startling resemblance to each other. They were like something out of an Arthurian legend— enchanted siblings who had been doomed into a profane and idyllic love. Many found it a bit eerie; but not the habitues of 120 Mount—and certainly not Michael Cooper.

I recall the circumstances of this photograph, which is one of his very first pictures of them. It was at Robert's and they were gamboling about the place, as young lovers are wont, and Michael blazing away with his Nikon, when they came to a momentary stop in the middle of the room; and Robert, lolling in his big Eames, raised his head with a mischievous twinkle and said, "Well now, Brian, you must let the girl know how you truly feel about her!" whereupon Brian, with typical randy cheekiness, had gingerly tickled the palm of her hand with the tip of his finger—resulting in probably the best, most characteristically animated photograph ever taken of the legendary Anita Pallenberg.

TERRY:

Now, here's one of the great pics. I know at least two interpretations have been advanced regarding this pic: one, that Mick has just entered and is trying to close the door very quietly so as not to disturb you and your muse; or two, that he is locking the door preparatory to drug abuse or at least smoking hemp. What is your view?

KEITH:

Trying to sneak out, I shouldn't wonder.

TERRY:

To take his pleasure with groupie-poon stashed in the corridor?

KEITH:

Somethin' o' that, absolutely.

TERRY:

Another common practice in those days, by all accounts.

KEITH:

I'm afraid so, yes.

TERRY:

Well, no one ever said the Stones were perfect.

KEITH:

this must be '66—I met Michael in late '65, and '66. And that is a '66 dulcimer in the front of the picture there. There's Michael, too. You can see him leaning out in his I-got-myself-in-the-picture mode, trying not to be in it. I might suggest that this person at the front here is Mike Gruber—famous for his cock impression . . . also did a spot of driving.

TERRY:

Now, how can Michael be in the shot there?

KEITH:

Well, because it's in a three-way mirror. Michael inadvertently got caught and just realized that he's also in it, and he is doing that great lean-back shot he's so famous for.

ANITA:

mick was always a showman—the front man—and he was always brilliant . . . his rhythm, appearance—he was always so sexy, shaking his tambour-ines—always laughing, always dancing, always *doing* something on stage—nonstop—with his maracas, different tambourines, shaking 'em all the time, dancing up and down—"Mr. Tambourine Man."

TERRY:

What's all this lot? Has an aura of substance abuse, perhaps derangement.

KEITH:

Should have; we were blasted that day.

ANITA:

that's Nicky Kramer—he was a lost soul. He just kind of wandered onto this scene—probably high on acid and never came down, I think, to this day— just lost, you know. He was like one of these upper-class penniless people who'd pounce on everybody—he wasn't good news, really.

KEITH:

and this is Mamouhd—Robert's Moroccan houseboy at the time . . . used to crash Robert's cars!

KEITH:

and there's Strawberry Bob [Robert Fraser] on the left—Spanish Tony, Chrissie, and Bill "Pussy Pink" Willis was there, too, I seem to recall. But that might be David Litvinoff in there as well. It was definitely either him or his buddy who sprung the police bust at Redlands. Here, though, I guess we'd decided to go on a wander from Redlands around West Wittering. Never mind wandering around the village—I think we did a tour of the whole South Downs that day!

KEITH:

More wandering—that was a long way from the village. What were we doing way up there? Why did we go there? Jane's place nearby maybe . . .

Jane Rainey? I don't know, don't ask me—I was on acid! I remember events from a little later on that day!

Incredible thing about Michael. I mean, he was looning about as much as the rest of us, and I couldn't have picked up a guitar and played in that state, but he kept the camera loaded, too! Kept it in focus, I mean; he was still working as well!

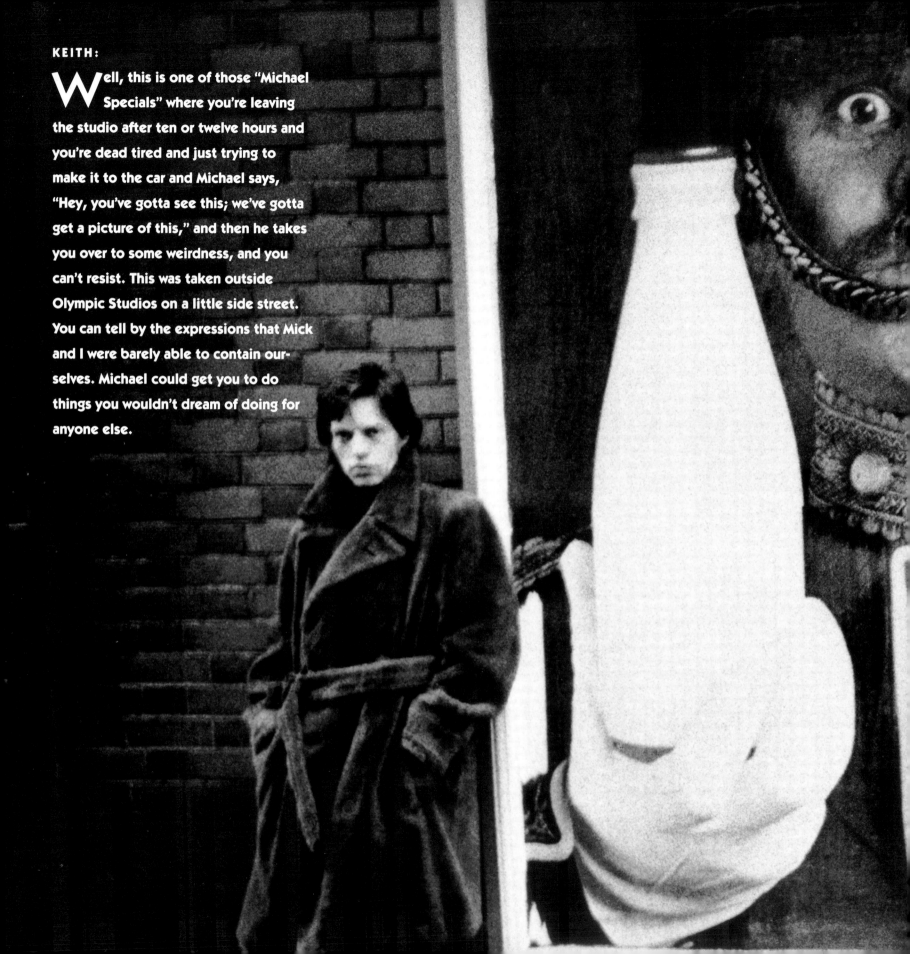

KEITH:

Well, this is one of those "Michael Specials" where you're leaving the studio after ten or twelve hours and you're dead tired and just trying to make it to the car and Michael says, "Hey, you've gotta see this; we've gotta get a picture of this," and then he takes you over to some weirdness, and you can't resist. This was taken outside Olympic Studios on a little side street. You can tell by the expressions that Mick and I were barely able to contain ourselves. Michael could get you to do things you wouldn't dream of doing for anyone else.

ANITA:

these jeans here are Keith's—these were sailor's jeans; he'd get two pairs, one pair was purple, the other one red, and he'd just cut them up—get some Scotch tape, sometimes leather, but just stick them together. His idea; he'd just do it himself.

KEITH:

Joshua Tree rocks. All getting very organic—must've been on mushrooms!

PERRY:

Michael told me that he went with you once to South America and he remembered pulling in to this tiny little village in Peru, where it turned out this kind of local music festival was going on . . . and they were all playing this totally unusual, hybrid style of music that you'd never even heard before. No one had heard of "The Stones" and you were all tired, exhausted—nowhere to stay—so you watched them playing for a bit, then took the guitar up there and just played their music back to them, spot on, adding all of these little touches of detail. And they were just literally stunned—amazed—couldn't believe that this gringo stranger could be playing their music so well!

KEITH:

Well, I have to thank my grandfather for that facility. He taught me to pick up the essentials of any kind of music. I mean, enough to astound the natives! Give me one run-through and I just pick up the essentials of it—I can do it with Indians and Japanese and anybody else. Brian was like that, too—and Ronnie as well. I can basically only do it on guitar—maybe put it up on piano now and again—but Brian could take any instrument and within half an hour he'd be playing it, getting something out of it— might not always be exactly what you're supposed to be getting out of it, but it'd be something good—something interesting that'd work. And Ronnie's the same—he can do it on anything and in that respect, too, very similar to Brian — and very strange, too, when you consider that he's sitting in, standing in Brian's old place. You know, except for Mick Taylor in between. But Ronnie has that same ability of being able to pick up on any instrument. In fact, just give him one run-through—boom, boom—it's part of his survival instincts probably! If this means that I get a bed tonight and something to eat. I'll get it down, you know! No problem.

KEITH:

ahh—Gram Parsons—when we were all up in Joshua Tree looking for UFO's. There was a barber chair just on the other side of those rocks. Some great loon had managed to put a working barber chair on top of the mountain, so you could goof on sunsets and sunrises and UFO's from the comfort of this revolving, adjustable chair, which I think Gram put us on to.

Gram probably did more than anybody to sort of put a new face on country music—I mean, the reason now you've got your Waylons and Willie Nelsons and why their music got accepted is probably more because of Gram than anybody. Country music up until that time—around the end of the '60s—was like just its own little backwater; he brought it into the mainstream of, you know, "Don't forget about this shit," and he brought all of those guys like Byrone Berline, et cetera, et cetera, into our circle, too.

KEITH:

More UFO's at Joshua Tree. You know, the person who I'm most pissed off about not still being around is Gram—with Michael running him a close second. I think that I probably learned more from Gram than anybody else.

KEITH:

So in the car there's Tony Phipps, Anita, and Phil Kaufman in the front. Still in California . . . Tony: "What's all this schmogg!" Phil Kaufman used to look after Gram and the Burrito Brothers; he's also the guy that stole Gram's body from the L.A. Airport mortuary. Him and a couple of mates hired a hearse, put some white coats on, took the coffin out of the airport, and took him out into the desert and burned him—'cause that's what Gram said: "If anything happens to me, don't let the family get my remains—just take me out in the desert and light it up." Which is what Phil did— got ninety days for it or something.

PERRY:

ere's Gram and Taj Mahal. Gram told this story about how the first time he met Taj, he was sitting at a table in a bar in the San Fernando Valley and Taj came in, this hulking great frame filling up the doorway, closely followed by his wife, who was even bigger than he was. They came straight over to Gram's table, and Taj picked him up off the ground, gave him a big bear hug, and said, "Man, it's great to see a white boy doing something!"

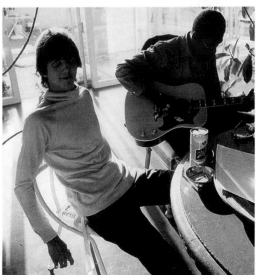

ANITA:

Gram arranged for us to go see this
show with Ray Charles and Tina
Turner—this one was in Las Vegas—he'd
always be doing things like that. I took
to Gram right away—he was just incredible—wonderful, handsome and smooth
and southern—and guitar player, the
lot—he was great—had the most beautiful voice—and he knew so many songs,
apart from all that he wrote—and he
used to just play.

ANITA:

I remember all these wires coming in through the kitchen window bringing the power in for the studio. The house had at least ten bedrooms, maybe more, and then other people started to come and rent houses there as well. And so slowly it became like the English invasion down in this little harbor at Villefranche.

It was a little pirate harbor, pirate village—which was like the deepest harbor in the Mediterranean, so there were all these warships there—Russian submarines, American submarines—

German, American navy, they were all there. It was, I suppose, one of their ports—you know, like the Sixth Fleet, they were always there . . . And on the other hand there was also Onassis, and Agnelli, and all those boats—they were all harbored there in the bay, and we had these huge binoculars set on the whole fucking scene! And we were just watching the whole bit, and then we started to get a bit braver and started

launching out into this bay—Keith bought a motorboat, this old speed-boat, and started just zooming around the bay, going out to these American destroyers, buzzing 'em. And I mean Keith drove a boat like he drove a car—you know, bouncing off trees, one prank after another—but he wouldn't listen . . . so I'd be on the shore or in the house, hands together, praying it didn't happen but just expecting him any min-ute to hit one of the boats or a metal marker or the jetty, just waiting for this explosion—you know, for the fuel to go up—but thank God by some miracle all that happened to him was he'd run out of gas. We'd hear this yelling from the bay. One of the boats would hand him down some fuel, or else we'd go out and rescue him.

ANITA:

People high on acid would decide to shoot out to the village; the whole thing was so crazy. There were these French cowboys that used to hang out outside the house and go up to people when they came out, and so they started to kind of put the pressure on us, so we'd give them little jobs, figured it'd be better to have them as friends. And then they came with drugs, as well. And it became a whole scene.

And I'd be having fits—every day there'd be twenty or thirty people to feed. I remember one time this tribe of Buddhist monks came—from Indonesia, I think, to put some particular kind of drumming on one of the tracks—stayed for days and days . . . and they'd be really quiet and genteel—very calm atmosphere about them. I remember them particularly sitting at the dining table, neatly arranged in their long,

flowing orange and yellow robes, very reposed, collected except that whenever any food was put on the table they became like animals. I mean, anything, everything that was put out on that table they'd literally ravage, demolish . . . whatever—however much you'd put out would just disappear in what seemed like just a few minutes. So I'd have my freakouts, too, you know—usually when I'd be halfway down the stairs, coming down in the morning to be greeted by this sea of twenty, thirty people, most of whom I didn't know, filling up our living room. I remember I'd scream at whoever it was, "Get out! Out!"—tossed anyone who wasn't part of the record out. And meanwhile Keith was coming up with all these fantastic songs for that record, which I think was really brilliant—pulling together all of those bits he'd put aside over the years—putting it together with all of this new inspiration.

KEITH:

that's Judy and Bobby Keys! Bobby was always kind of on my staff, even on this last Steel Wheels Tour. A whole brass section had been hired—good guys. But something wasn't happening, so I call Bobby: "Not getting any answers, Bobby, so just come up to New York. Just come to rehearsals . . . be there. I'll guarantee you." And that's basically what's always happened with Bobby.

TERRY:

this picture has a certain "south of France" aura. Isn't that where you made *Exile on Main Street*—considered by many to be the Stones' finest album?

KEITH:

Well, it was a very important album to us at that time. We were at a low point, with a lot of tax problems, and a good album was an absolute must for us. We figured the quickest way to do it would be to hole up somewhere and just, you know, do it. So we found the great house on Cap Ferrat near Villefranche, rented it for a couple of months, and set up a recording studio in the basement.

TERRY:

A very unorthodox setup by all accounts.

KEITH:

Yeah, it had huge commercial electric cables going across the patio and into the basement window. Somewhat un-sightly for a posh Riviera villa. The chicks didn't dig it—kept getting tripped up by the big cables.

117

TERRY:

now, about these Stonehenge pics . . .

KEITH:

These Stonehenge pics were part of a period of Visiting Famous Places While Whacked Out. We'd drop a little sunshine, pile into the old Bentley, slip an Otis Redding 45 into the deck, and head for the hills, or the desert . . . or wherever.

TERRY:

I suppose your infamous pilgrimage to Joshua Tree might fall into that category . . .

KEITH:

Absolutely. I think it was Gram who laid that trip on for us. We went out there to watch the UFO's. And maybe take a spin in one, should the occasion arise.

ANITA:

Yeah, we just decided to go—we'd been at a club where Gram was playing; he was with the Byrds then—and we kind of just took him away and went down there. But these clothes . . . I mean, that was our normal getup, to go out in London.

KEITH:

Joshua Tree at dawn. Geronimo awakes!

ANITA:

It's always built up that Brian was kicked out of the band, but I've always thought that it was the other way around. Brian really was always a rhythm and blues man, and that's it. He'd take me to so many places where blues players'd hang out. One time, for instance, it'd be the second floor of some building in Oxford Street and he'd introduce me to Eric Clapton and all of those guys, and they'd just play this great music so beautifully, so powerfully. That's why he took to the rhythm and music of Jujuku. He was such an extraordinary character, really. But he didn't like what the Stones were doing with all of that Satanic Majesty shit—and he also didn't agree with all that kind of hippy "we love you" stuff—and on top of that he was also suffering terrible fits of clinical paranoia. So all of that was going on with him at the same time. And he also wasn't aware that the drugs he was taking were just compounding the situation—making it worse—but then, I mean, who is, when you're in it? But, I mean, he was never into heavy drugs—just alcohol and pills; by then he'd also stopped taking acid. I think when he went to a concert with Jimi Hendrix and someone took the shot of him with all the beads and flowers and everything, he was on acid then . . . but by then we'd fallen out anyway. I do know he was never into heroin—in fact, wasn't even smoking—because apart from anything else he was too paranoiac. But, yeah, obviously the acid didn't help at all, not at all—and he wasn't aware of it, that it was making it worse, not for quite a while. When you're in it you don't realize . . . you just haven't got a choice, really. His whole lifestyle had deteriorated. There were a lot of people around him who just weren't of his level. They were around him just to use him. He was bloated, always apologizing. Basically, he was surrounded by these Neanderthal types, and that certainly didn't help his paranoia. I mean, they really resented him. But then later, he was very creative again. Alexis Korner had got in touch with him, and they were going to form another band, a blues band. He had regained his vision, but physically he was still recovering. And John Lennon also then was talking to him about forming a band. Apart from anything else they both had this same kind of "up-front thing." So basically, I think he was in a lot better shape by then—just having the odd glass of wine. Looking at this photograph, that's what's so sad and quite frankly still so suspicious about his death.

131

mick Taylor was basically always very true to himself. He didn't like all that star stuff, wasn't very impressed by it—just played his guitar and that was it. He got fed up with being subject to all the nonsense, so he split . . . but the bad thing that did happen to him was that he got into the junk, too—and suffered a lot through that. The Stones did bring quite a few people down—to a certain extent, anyway. Not that it was really their fault, because everyone chooses what they want to do, but there was that whole environment, the parties, and Keith doing what he was doing, and some of them got stuck and went under. But I think Mick Taylor's quite happy now—he's been through quite a few things—and I think now, maybe, he's got a few regrets about leaving the Stones. He thought he had a good thing going, but at the time everything was getting too much.

TERRY:

I believe this is the concert for Brian at Hyde Park after his death. What do you remember about it?

KEITH:

I mostly remember how Ronnie and I kept bumping into each other. We were both sort of wandering around behind the stands—like trying to be alone, I guess. It was weird, because my impulse was to ask him right there if he would join the band, but I thought maybe it was too soon after Brian's death. Later on I found out that Ronnie wanted to ask me but was thinking the same thing about it being too soon.

TERRY:

And didn't Mick read a poem at the concert?

KEITH:

He read Shelley's "Ode to Peace."

TERRY:

And then a lot of butterflies were released. What was all that in aid of, if one may ask?

KEITH:

What, the butterflies? Well, butterflies were very important in our getting out of the Redlands drug bust, you know. Just when things were looking darkest, some hip young writer at the *Times* wrote this very moving editorial about our situation called "Who Would Break a Butterfly on the Wheel?" And it created such sympathy for us and resentment towards the authorities that we were let off. The case was dropped.

KEITH:

Oh, look at this—Cecil Beaton in Marrakesh! This one's appeared in a magazine. It showed just the top of the shot; had a caption to it. Cecil had said something like, "*Wonderful* head and torso!"

TERRY:

I must say you're looking quite relaxed in this one.

KEITH:

Just giving the old head a breather.

KEITH:

morocco . . . that was the first time I went there. Brion Gysin knew various of the local tribes—lived in Tangiers. It was through talking to Gysin that Brian did that Jujuku record—he took some equipment up there, listened to the pipes of Pan, which they do once a year.

ANITA:

That's Robert at the entrance to Sidi Mamoun—Paul and Talleedtha Getty's place.

The first time I met Robert was at a rather stuffy reception in London—the surroundings were very grand, the place filled with Lords and Lady doo-dahs, and there, across the room, was this guy in a bright green suit, green shirt, green tie, green shoes, and his fly open. "That's someone I've got to meet!" I thought.

TERRY:

This was the period when I hadn't seen Anita for a while and she said, "Robert raped me!"—but she said it gleefully!

MARIANNE:

Robert had a whole period of that, you know—he almost pulled me one night. It was really nice and we were having a wonderful time and—just . . . you know, it was very slow and it was sort of kissing and very nice . . . genteel—*almost*, you know, that's an awful word, but . . . then Mick walked in.

Actually, I was quite relieved and I think Robert was, too. It was like a beautiful minute, you know—with touches of sexuality in it. It wasn't real, you know; I still can't quite imagine making love with Robert. Anyway, I never did.

AL DIA SIGUIENTE...

CLIFF ROBERTSON · RED BUTTONS
IRINA DEMICK · MARIUS GORING

artistas invitados
BRODERICK CRAWFORD · JAMES ROBERTSON JUSTICE

Director:
ROBERT PARRISH

CinemaScope

Guión:
HOWARD CLEWES

CINE ROXY

ANITA:

traveling was wonderful—it was new. We'd fly to L.A. for a party, go to different parts of the world, bring different things back, put different cultures together.

At one point, though, it started to become pretty obvious that Andrew had done his work too well. I mean, I remember one time Brian and I had been staying in Tangiers and we pinched this little rose bowl—washing bowl—from the hotel. Well, I happened—for some rea-

son, I don't know why—to be carrying it in my arm when we got off the plane and out of customs. Next morning, banner headlines: "Brian Jones and actress Anita Pallenberg return from Africa with satanic rituals." Utter nonsense.

MARIANNE:

We'd just got off the bust—they'd let Mick out. So we thought that the place to go and hide at first was Braziers, my father's place, which was a country house in Oxfordshire. And indeed, they never found us.

TERRY:

I asked Mick Jagger what this picture was all about, and he said, "It's about a right bloody balls-up, that's what it's about." Fairly shouted it, he did. Would you say it's a good characterization of the pic?

KEITH:

Absolutely. That's the incident that the press went berserk about. Like they thought we should be drawn and quartered—and then kicked about on the ground, I suppose.

TERRY:

What was the nature of the complaint?

KEITH:

Well, it was all too ridiculous, really. I mean, we'd been driving all afternoon in the old Bentley, stopped at this petrol station for a fill-up, and decided to have a pee while we were there. Well, the guy said the toilet was out of order, so we were having a discreet pee against a stone wall sort of behind the station. The guy freaks out, calls the constabulary, and the next thing it's in all the London papers—big stories about the Stones urinating in public, defacing private property, and all that lot bloody banner headlines.

TERRY:

Lucky, I suppose, they didn't have you up for indecent exposure.

KEITH:

Exactly. What bloody rubbish.

ANITA:

I don't think Keith got too involved with the Maharishi. I certainly didn't see him coming—he suddenly appeared—but I just kind of ignored the whole thing.

161

KEITH:

The Tantric Art thing was the only thing that interested me really in those days. I mean, I had no time to meditate then; I still don't find much time, really. Don't know about you lot! I strayed from the path, I admit it.

If someone is involved in what's going on around them, they aren't gonna get caught up by a bunch of Indian hustlers. If you're looking for a guru, forget it—they find you, you don't find them—a guru looks for his fucking apprentice. One day somebody'll tap me on the shoulder and it'll be a bloke in a turban saying "You!" and until that happens I'll forget it—you know, I've got too much else to take care of, quite honestly.

ANITA:

I got involved with the film *Performance* right from the beginning, because I knew Donald Cammell and used to hang out with him before. I remember when we were writing the script together in St. Tropez and the pages all flew into the sea and we had to run in and gather them all back again—and then he was getting on with it, organizing it with the producer and all of that, and then suddenly they asked me, would I like to do it. Warner Brothers had wanted Tuesday Weld for the film, but Deborah [Dixon], Donald's girlfriend, had managed to break her back—it was just one of those things—and so she was laid up for a year. I'd always felt more like part of creating the story and all of this, and I thought, "Well, that's that"—but then it came down to playing it, so then for me it was pretty much down-to-home stuff.

KEITH:

Stupid bitch. I'll always love her, just **S** can't live with her.

TERRY:

But you never felt *threatened* by punk—punk-rock . . . and heavy metal—that they might be doing something *beyond* where you were at?

KEITH:

Beyond? No, no, no—*louder* maybe . . . or maybe not even that; maybe it just seems louder, because you usually hear them in smaller places. But anyway, it's not really a musical thing, is it? I mean it's not even an audio thing—it's a personality thing . . . an attitude. People don't go to *hear* them, they go to *see* them . . . to see what manner of outrage they might be up to . . . like this one guy I heard about was eating tambourines on stage. First I thought they said "tangerine," so I wasn't too impressed, but it was *tam*-bourine . . . he got right sick from all accounts . . .

TERRY:

So you didn't find anything really new, or innovative, in the so-called "New Wave" music?

KEITH:

Well, I *did* hear about this one guy—with "The Slits," I think . . . or maybe it was "The Gashes"—who pissed straight into the middle of this monstro amp, and got electrocuted—had his back to the audience and it knocked him right out into the third row . . . I mean, I wouldn't've

TERRY:

Some observers have given you the title, somewhat mistakenly perhaps, father of punk . . . Rumor has it that you were within a whisker of writing a prepunk, heavy metal score for the film.

KEITH:

ANITA:

Keith was not exactly keen on my role with Mick in that movie—then Donald asked Keith to write the music for the film and he refused point-blank. And then Robert didn't help the situation much by renting out his flat in Mount Street to me for some exorbitant sum, on the production tab, and then forgetting to move out! So walking back into the atmosphere of that flat could be somewhat delicate at times, to put it mildly! Donald would reduce Mick to tears over not coming up with the right piece of music or the feeling that he wanted for a scene, and then to tears of joy when he finally hit it! Mick and I would both be terrified by one of his "Von Sternberg" type tirades and rages—but when we all got it right it was great. Even through all of that, Donald and Keith still remained friends.

ANITA:

and there's Keith . . . The volcano **a**waits!

KEITH:

the volcano awaits Madam's return.

173